AF406283

Contents

A Lonely Walk
By: Olga Foreign

A Lonely Walk
By: Olga Foreign

A Lonely Walk
By: Olga Foreign

Self

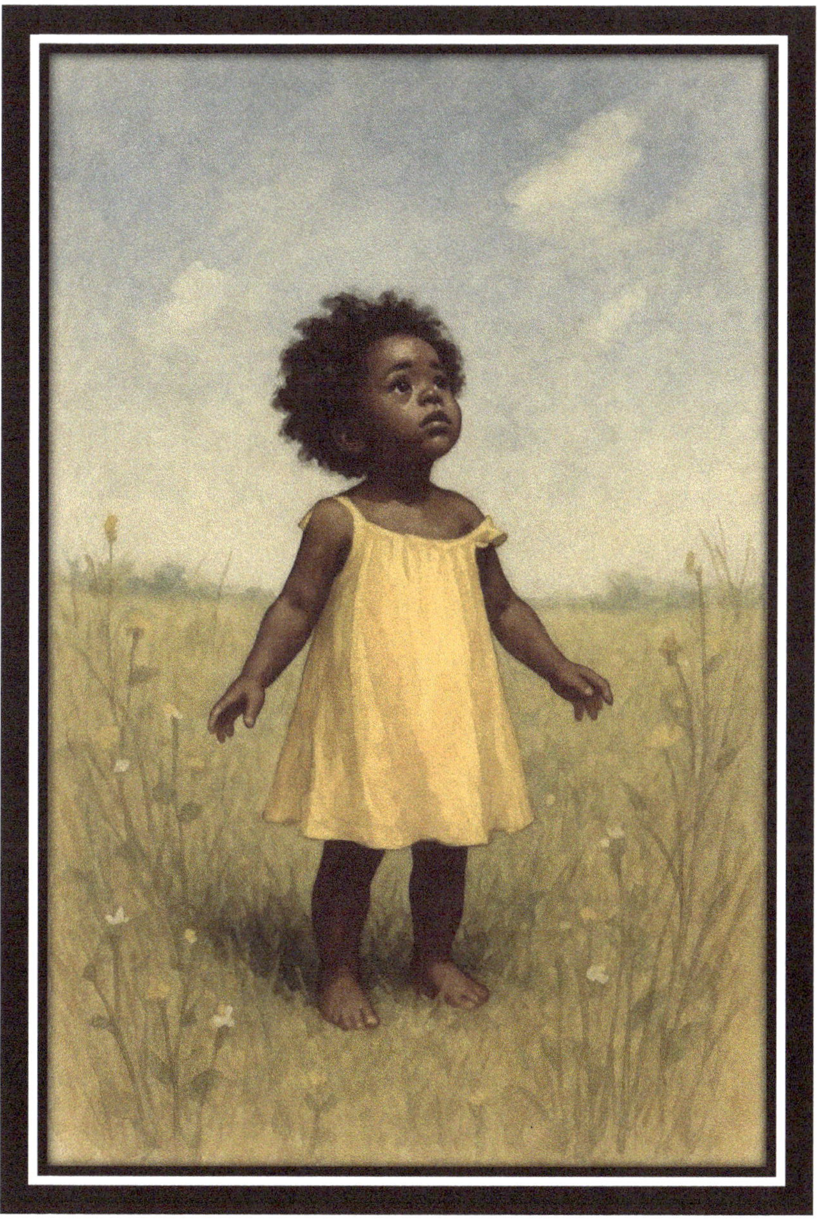

A Lonely Walk
By: Olga Foreign

Before She Knew Time Sickness

Before she knew time sickness was at hand
She danced in glee, willing to hold anyone's hands
Stranger, shadow, or storm.
With sunshine on her brow
And a song escaping her lips,
The little girl in the yellow dress
Danced and skipped and skipped and skipped

The world was wide then
But not too wide.
It fit inside her laughter,
Folded into sidewalk chalk and sticky palms,
Into dandelion wars and questions without answers.

She didn't yet count hours.
She didn't yet carry names.
Now she
She believed people stayed, dreams waited,
and growing up meant growing more free.

But time has teeth.
And sickness wears a watch.
Now she – now I –
Know the price of knowing.
Of building.
Of Branding silence into something the world respects.

Still sometimes I hear her.
Not in the clock, but in the wind.
Not in the to do list, but in the lull between tasks.

And when I do –
I skip, just once, for her, for me
For the girl in the yellow dress
Before time ever touched her shoulder.

A Lonely Walk
By: Olga Foreign

Barriers

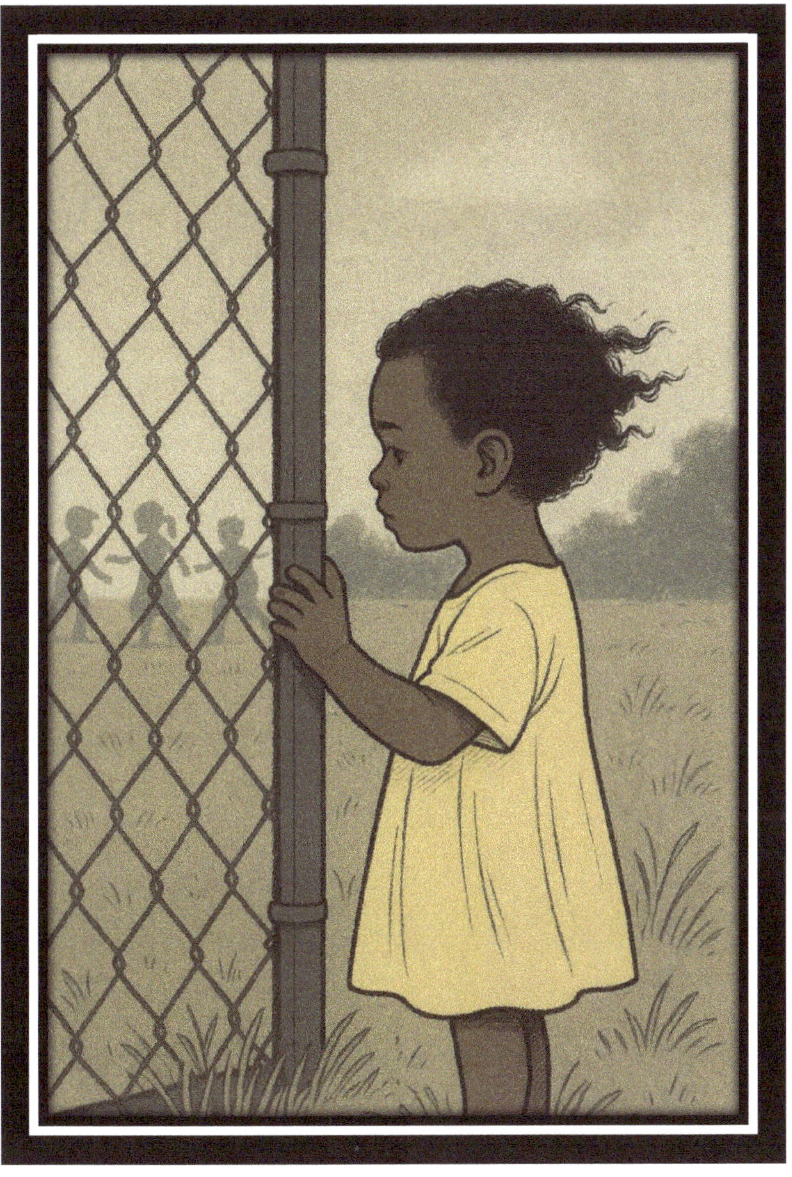

A Lonely Walk
By: Olga Foreign

Still, We Are

We don't have to prove it anymore.
Not our worth.
Not our genius.
Not our right to exist.

Still — we are.

They told us we were once
but never now.
Told us our golden age
was back then,
over there,
buried.
But here we are.
Not just surviving —
being.

Being loud, soft,
brilliant, broken,
healing, human.
Being more than what they counted,
measured, or predicted.

We are not waiting for permission.
We are not asking for space.
We are the space.
The presence.
The proof.
The pulse.
Still, we are breath.
Still we are body.
Still we are spirit
untouched by census or system.

Still, we are here.
And **we are not leaving**

A Lonely Walk
By: Olga Foreign

Inward

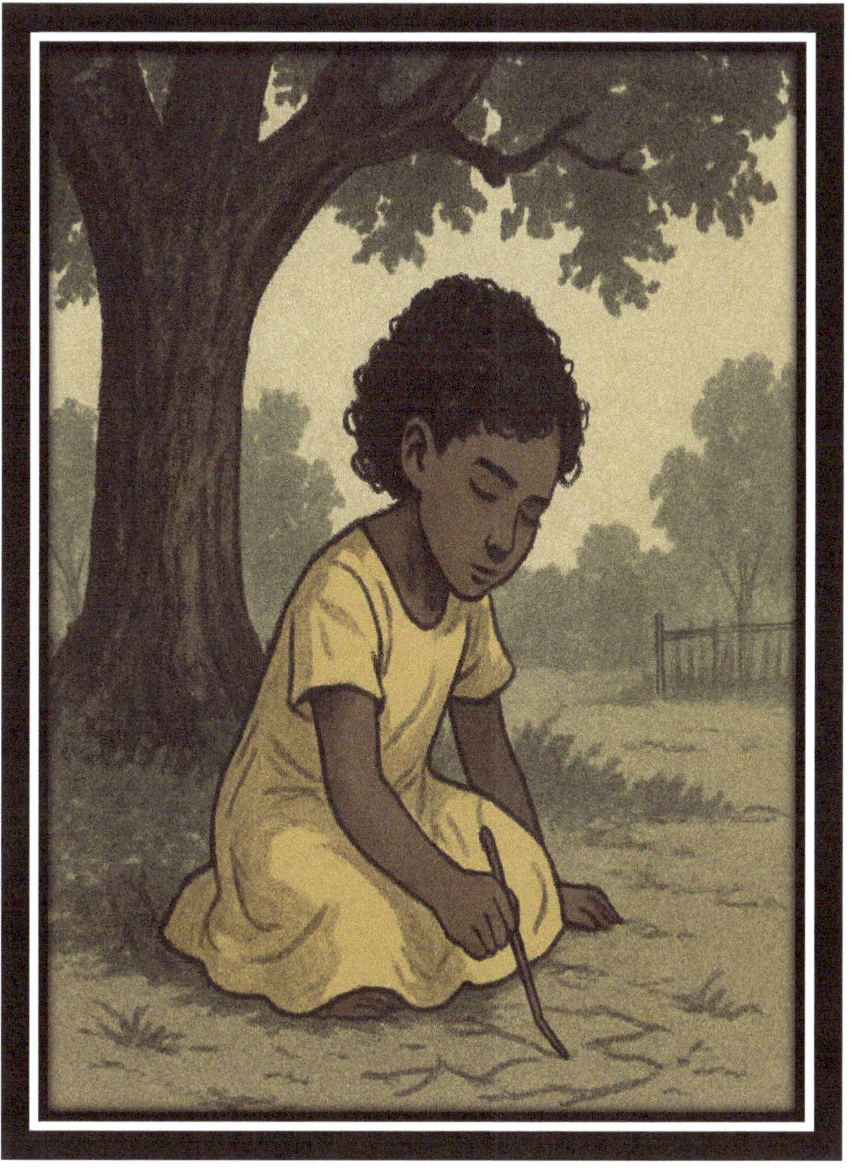

A Lonely Walk
By: Olga Foreign

Return From Love?

They talk about love
like it's a door you can reopen.
Like healing is guaranteed
if you *just believe hard enough.*

But some of us…
never made it back.

Some of us were taught
love meant control.
Love meant silence.
Love meant giving parts of yourself
that never grew back.

We were born in households
where "I love you"
was followed by a bruise.
Or worse —
a cold room
where no one came to find you.

They say love is a light,
but what if your first flame
was a fire that burned the house down?

Some of us locked love out
because the last time we let it in
it *took everything.*

Some of us are museums now —
full of beauty,
guarded by glass,
"look, but don't touch."

A Lonely Walk
By: Olga Foreign

And people say:
"Why are you so guarded?"
Because the last time I opened
they stole my blueprint.

Some hearts
don't get rebuilt.
Some hearts survive
with scaffolding and caution tape.

And that's still love —
just not the kind you sing about.

It's the love of *not being touched.*
Of walking away early.
Of setting boundaries so high
you forget what's on the other side.

They say everyone can be healed.
But what if healing
is a luxury you weren't taught to afford?

Some of us stay broken —
not because we want to,
but because we've survived
by staying *unreachable.*

So don't judge the fortress.
It was built
after the fire.

A Lonely Walk
By: Olga Foreign

Thoughts

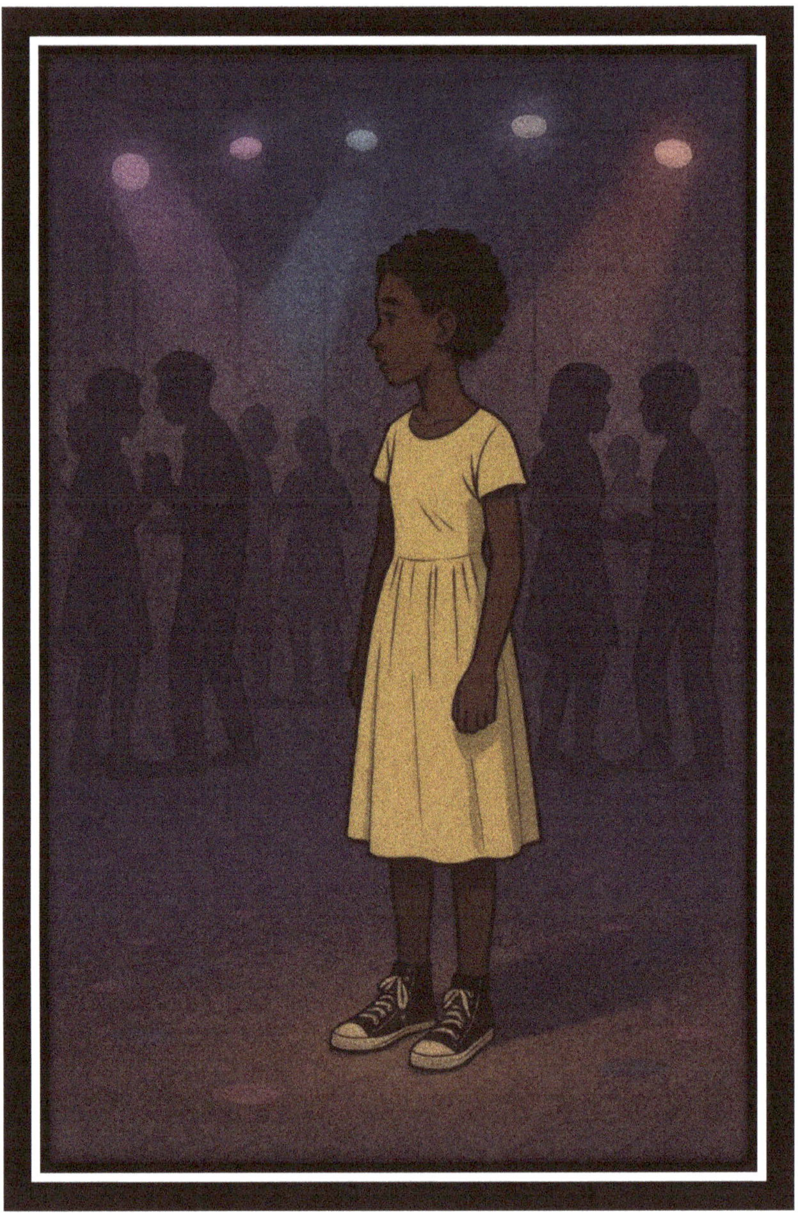

A Lonely Walk
By: Olga Foreign

Holy Questions

They said,
*"Be quiet in church,
don't ask why.
Your answers come later —
like after you die."*

But I got questions
burning like light:
Why does **God** only talk
to folks dressed in white?

Why do they say
"you're too young to know,"
but they teach me about sin
before I learn how to grow?

Why's the pastor so rich
while my mom works two shifts?
Why do blessings feel bought,
and the poor get skipped?

They say
"God is love" —
but they punish with fear.
They say *"God is near"* —
but I don't feel Him here.

They preach from books
that erased my skin.
They show me a heaven
that won't let me in
unless I fit rules
they made up last week,

A Lonely Walk
By: Olga Foreign

and pray in a voice
that's not mine when I speak.

I believe in spirit,
in wind, in flame —
but I don't need a building
to call His name.

So, I ask,
and they frown.
I doubt, and they pause.
But truth don't need silence
to prove its cause.

So, I'll walk with my questions.
I'll pray in my way.
And if God's real —
He can hear me anyway.

A Lonely Walk
By: Olga Foreign

Given

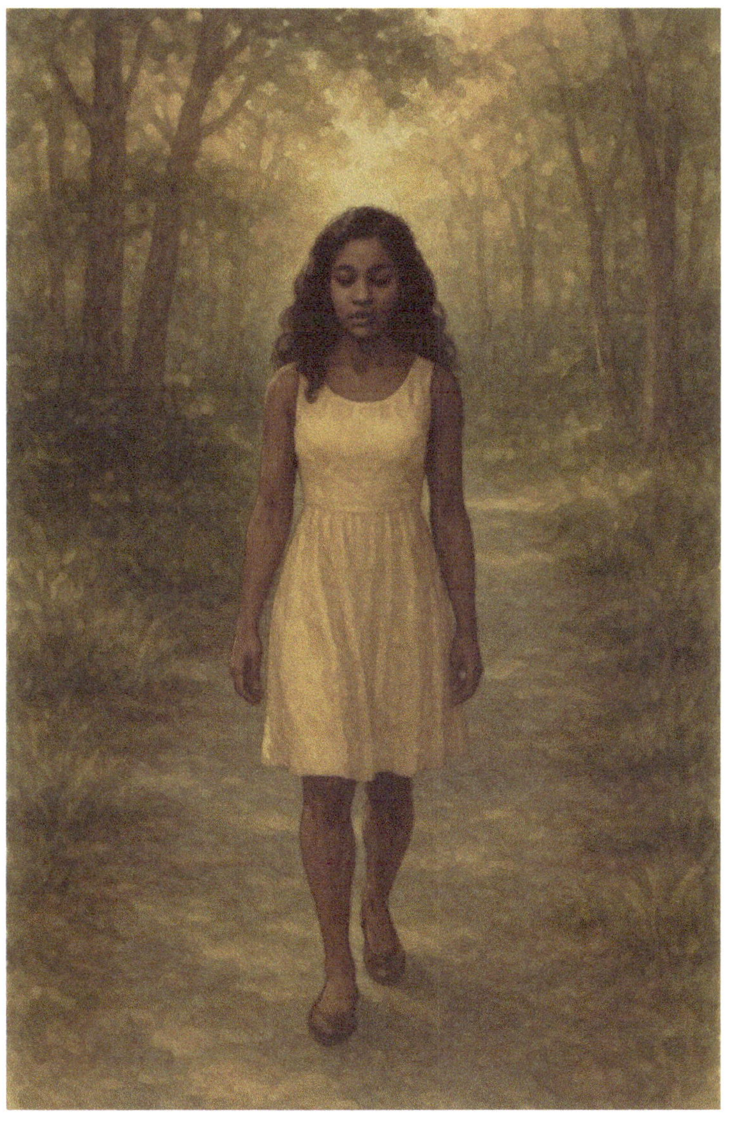

A Lonely Walk
By: Olga Foreign

You Can't Own This

You think you own it
because your name's on a deed?
Because a paper says "yours"
after you planted a seed?
You didn't make this.
Didn't shape the cliff.
Didn't carve the canyon
or stir the mist.

You didn't place the stars
that pull the tides.
Didn't build the soil
where the tree still hides
its sacred language.

You showed up
with fence posts and flags.
We showed up
with prayers and patience.

You called it a "claim."
We called it a **gift.**

And when we shared it,
you mistook generosity
for ignorance.

But land is not yours
just because you got here loud.
It's not a possession.
It's a parent.
And you don't inherit the earth —
you *borrow it.*

A Lonely Walk
By: Olga Foreign

You can't own a sky
you didn't paint.
You can't sell a river
you didn't name.

You walk on bones
and call it real estate.

But the land knows.
It remembers your footprints.
It remembers the treaties broken,
the fires started,
the names scraped from its stones.

And one day,
the ground will speak again —
not in court,
but in **quakes.**

Because you cannot steal
what watches you bleed
and still grows back
without your help.

A Lonely Walk
By: Olga Foreign

First

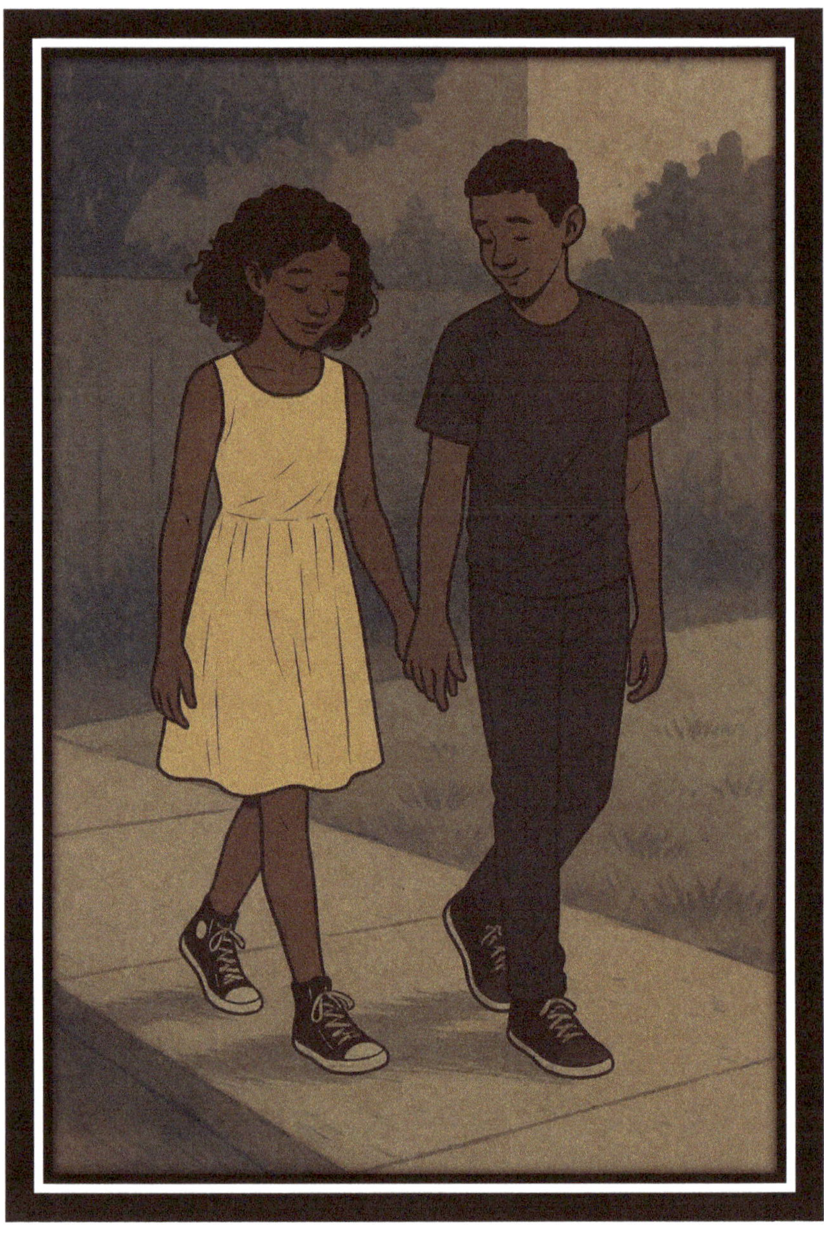

A Lonely Walk
By: Olga Foreign

Memory Speaks

I'm not a ghost,
but I've been hiding.
I'm not a book —
I'm who's been **guiding.**

They call me Memory,
but not the school kind.
Not dates and facts,
but what lives in your mind
when someone hums
a song you *feel* —
and you don't know why
but it feels real.

I live in grandma's quiet stare.
In how you braid
your sister's hair.
In dreams that make your chest feel tight
like someone's speaking through the night.

They tried to erase me.
Burned my pages.
Put your story
in other cages.

Taught you names
that weren't your own.
Taught you pride
in broken tone.

They said:
"Forget the past — it's gone."
But I've been *here*
this whole time long.

A Lonely Walk
By: Olga Foreign

I'm the reason you ask,
"Where am I from?"
I'm the echo that plays
like a beat on a drum.

Without me,
you're floating —
just guessing your way.
With me?
You walk
in a warrior's sway.

So when you feel lost,
just close your eyes.
I'm not a myth.
I don't wear disguise.

I'm Memory —
and I remember you.
Now it's your turn
to remember *too.*

A Lonely Walk
By: Olga Foreign

Time Madness

By: Olga Foreign

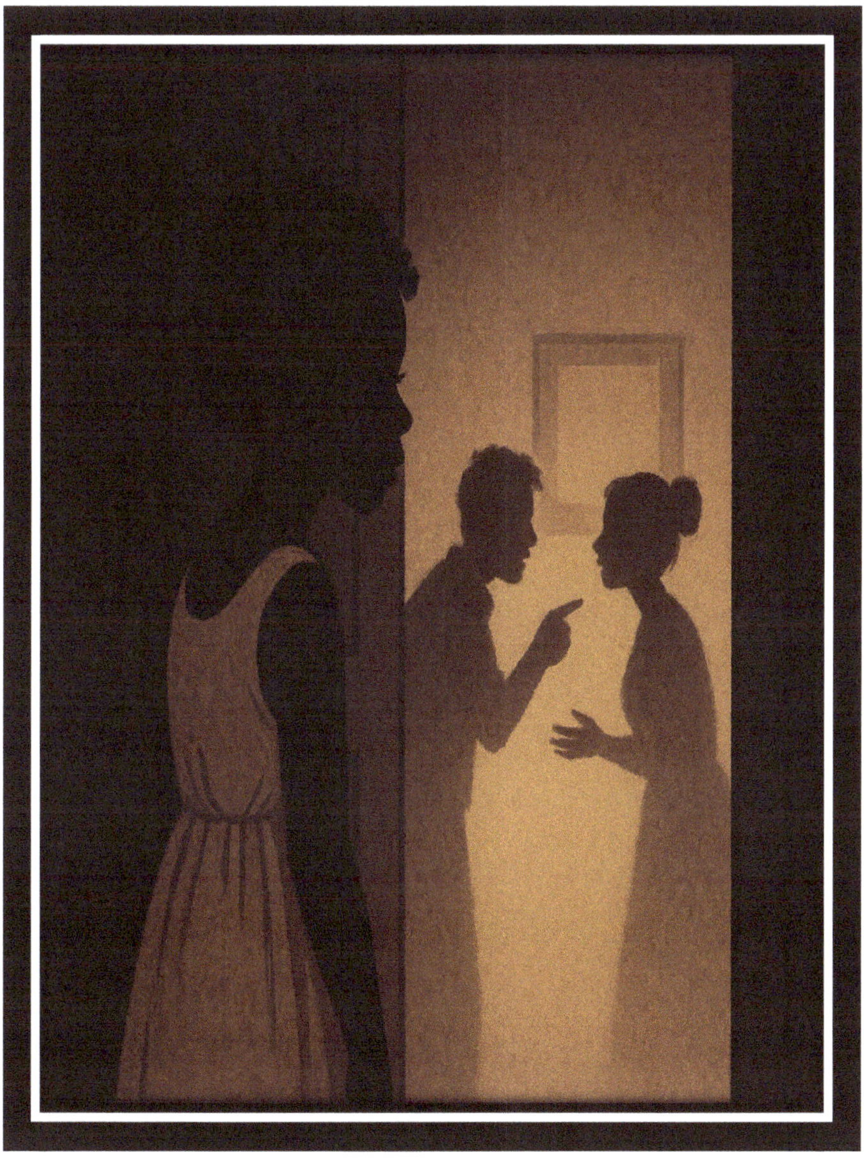

A Lonely Walk
By: Olga Foreign

The Skin They Sold Us

They said "you're white"
and gave you a prize —
but they never told you
that label was lies.

Before all that,
you were just you —
from a country, a village,
with stories and truth.

But they came with maps
and drew new lines.
Gave out colors
and sold new signs.

"White" became power.
"White" became rule.
They made it sound simple —
but you were the tool.

They told you,
"You're better — just look at your face."
But they never explained
why they needed a race
to keep folks divided,
to keep control,
to give some nothing
but call it a role.

See, whiteness ain't roots.
It's not where you're from.
It's a mask they gave out
so the system could run.

A Lonely Walk
By: Olga Foreign

It won't feed your soul.
It won't give you peace.
It just makes you feel "full"
while the hunger increase.

So listen, young one —
be smarter than hate.
Unlearn what they taught you
before it's too late.

Your worth ain't skin.
It's how you move.
It's how you treat people.
It's what you prove.

You don't need whiteness
to feel like more.

You just need truth
and a soul that roars.

A Lonely Walk
By: Olga Foreign

Me, In Your Eyes

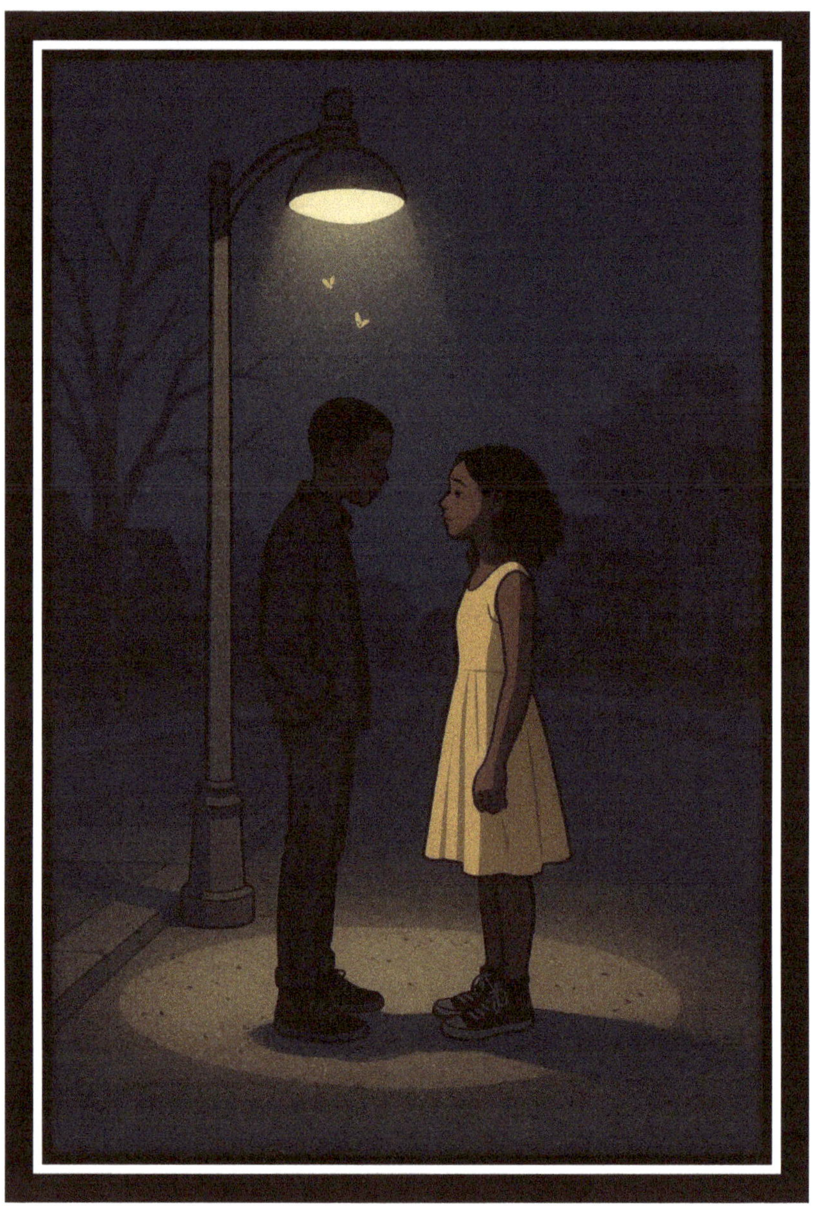

A Lonely Walk
By: Olga Foreign

Ode to Rap

You tried to silence us —
so we rhymed instead.
Put pain to a beat
and bled through the thread.

You banned our books,
cut funds from the schools —
so we picked up a mic
and rewrote the rules.

We didn't have violins,
so we looped our cries.
Turned bass into heartbeat,
truth into highs.

We rhymed hunger.
We rhymed grief.
We turned rage
into something with teeth.

We spoke in metaphors
because they wouldn't hear us plain.
Now the whole world moves
to the rhythm of our *pain.*

You called it noise —
then stole the sound.
Took the crown,
but not the **ground.**

Because rap ain't fashion.
It's field report.
It's poetry with a passport
and court support.

A Lonely Walk
By: Olga Foreign

It told the stories
the news ignored.
Turned block parties
into global lore.

We ain't just artists —
we're *historians with flow.*
Griots with headphones.
Resistance on show.

And no matter how much you censor or spin it —
as long as we breathe,
we're still in it.

This is the voice
you couldn't chain.
This is rap.
It doesn't whisper.
It reigns.

A Lonely Walk
By: Olga Foreign

Your Eyes Closed

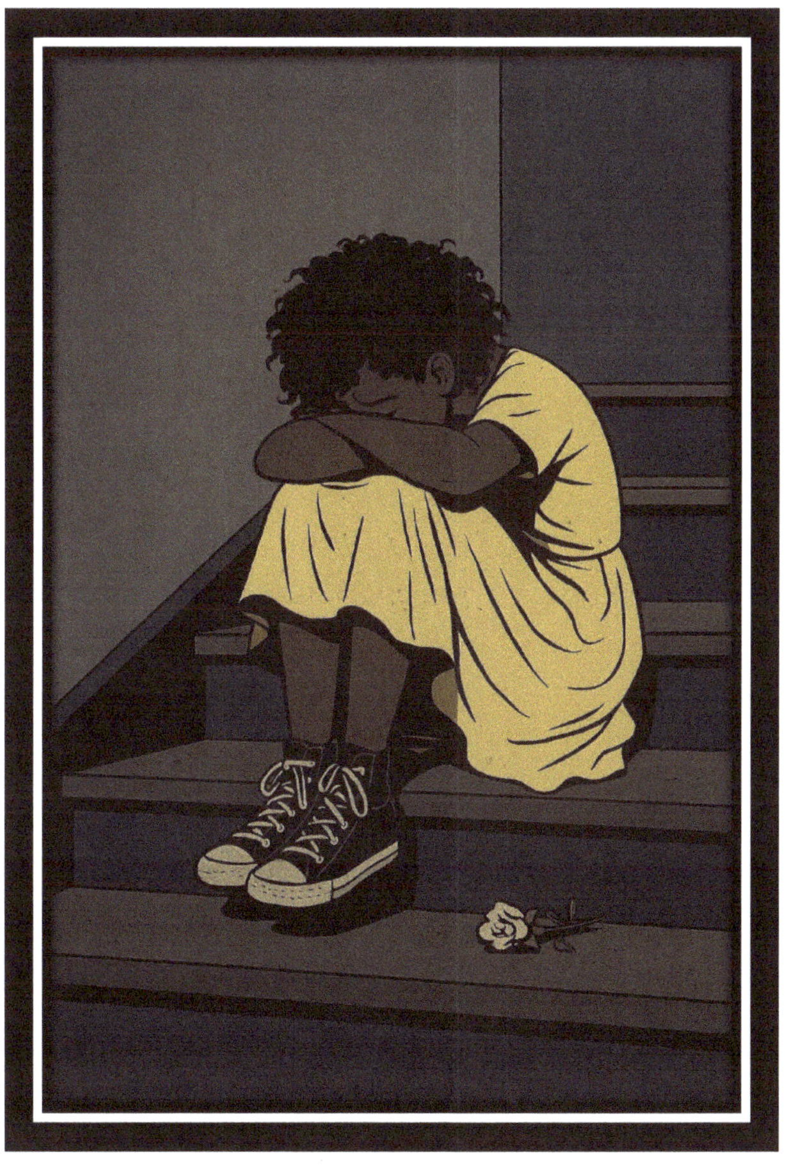

A Lonely Walk
By: Olga Foreign

Cage Comfort

The door was open.
For years.
For lifetimes.

But I didn't leave.

Not because I liked it here,
but because out there?
No one promised it'd be better.
Only different.

And different is terrifying
when you've mastered survival.

In this cage, I knew the rules.
I knew the hours.
I knew how much of me to shrink
so I wouldn't get hurt.

Out there?
What if I grew
and got cut down again?

What if freedom isn't safety —
just a prettier version
of the same pain?

So, I stayed.

I decorated my bars.
Hung art on the walls of my limits.
Made peace with the silence
so it wouldn't scream back at me.

A Lonely Walk
By: Olga Foreign

Because when your whole life
has been convincing yourself you're fine —
you forget
that "fine" is just a fancier word for *stuck.*

And maybe that's the real prison:

Not the walls,
but the lie that says
you're safer inside them.

A Lonely Walk
By: Olga Foreign

Belonging

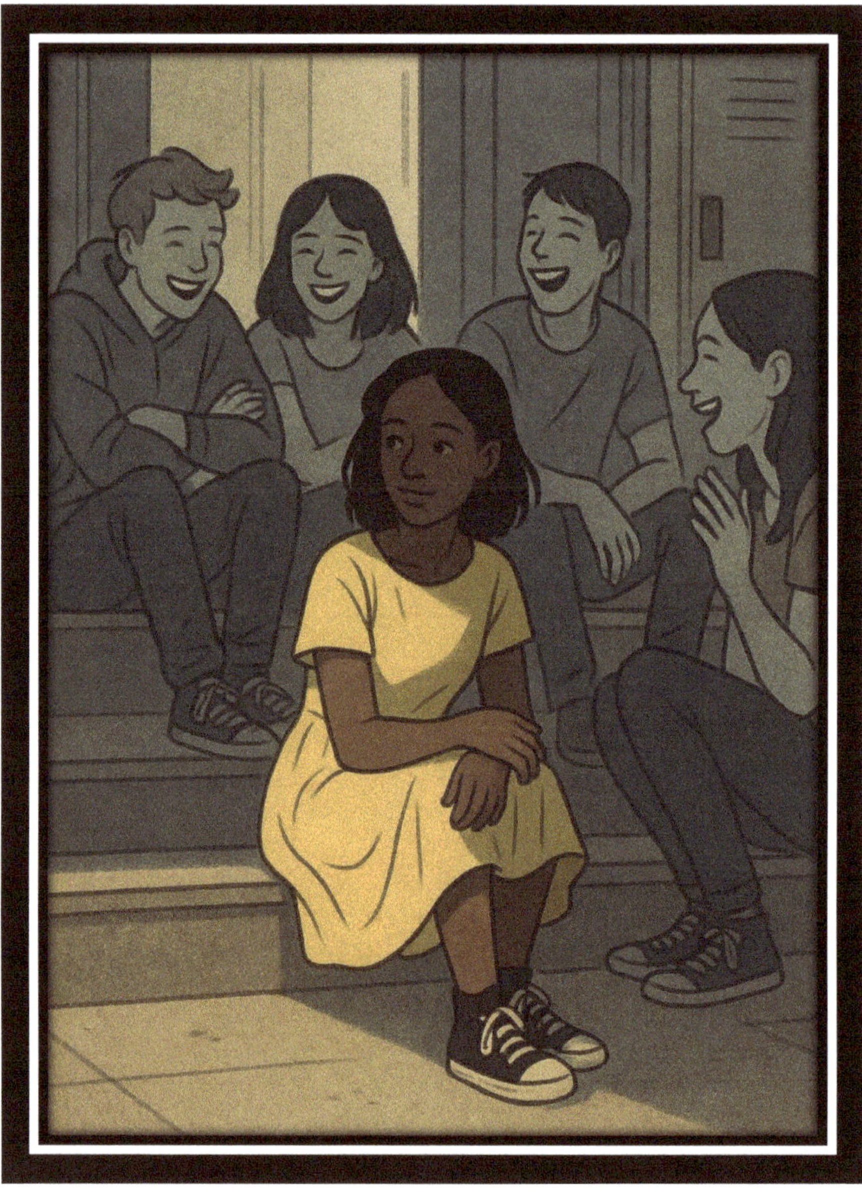

A Lonely Walk
By: Olga Foreign

The Imprisoned Mind

They told me I was free.
And I believed them
because I could walk outside.
Because I wasn't in chains.
Because I wasn't hanging from a tree.
But no one told me
freedom had a *definition.*

And no one asked
if I even knew what it felt like
to breathe
without checking the air first.

They gave me "choices" —
but never gave me *truth.*
Taught me how to vote,
but not how to question
the question itself.

I've been surviving so long,
freedom sounds like a fairy tale.
A luxury.
A trick word wrapped in anthem.

They said I was free —
but I've been raised by systems
that shrink you
for speaking,
for resting,
for dreaming outside the grid.

And if I'm honest…
I've never really seen freedom.
Only the *stories about it.*

A Lonely Walk
By: Olga Foreign

The stories where it's earned
by becoming
something I'm not.

So, what am I chasing?
What is freedom
to a mind
born in a cage
with velvet walls
and national flags?
They told me to be brave —
but all I've known is permission.
All I've learned is limits.

And now I wonder:
What if the real revolution
isn't running out of the cage —
but **realizing you were never supposed to be in one?**

A Lonely Walk
By: Olga Foreign

3X = X

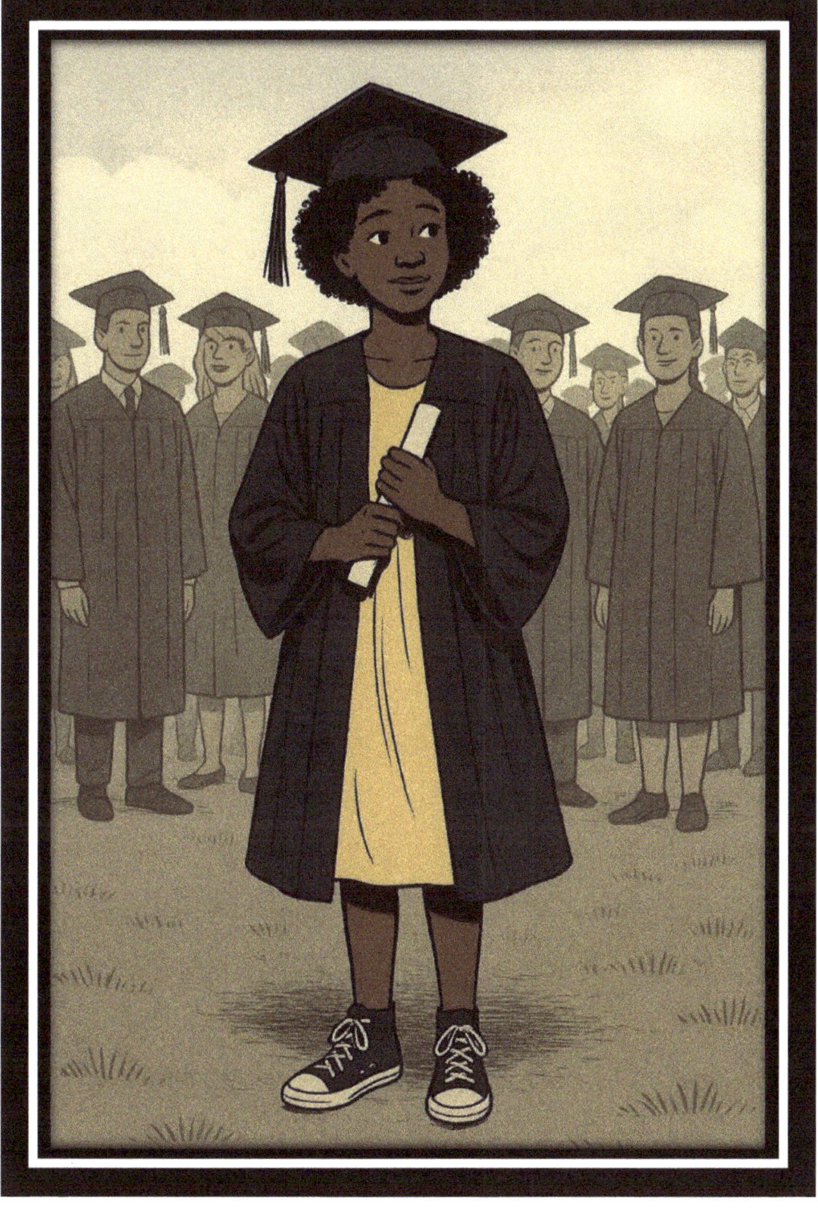

A Lonely Walk
By: Olga Foreign

The Prison I Carry

The cage isn't out there.
It's not a building.
Not a border.
Not a flag I didn't choose.
It's here.
Inside this skin.
Inside the breath I hold
when I want to speak but don't.

I'm not trapped in a place.
I'm trapped in a *state*
— physical, mental, spiritual —
a space between knowing
and never having known.

I'm scared of what's beyond me
because I don't know what's within me.
What if I walk out there
and meet a version of myself
I was never allowed to become?

What if I was never taught how to want?
Or love?
Or be
without apology?

I lost my memories,
my roots,
my right to say "this is who I am."

So how do I leave a prison
when I don't even know
where *freedom* begins?

A Lonely Walk
By: Olga Foreign

Maybe I'm not staying
because I like it here —
maybe I stay
because it's the only place
that doesn't expect me to know
what was taken from me.

And that's the worst kind of stolen —
the kind where you can't even name
what you lost.

So, I sit.
In a cage with no lock.
In a life with no map.
In a body I don't fully understand.

Not because I'm weak.
But because no one ever told me
I was allowed
to go find
me.

A Lonely Walk
By: Olga Foreign

Adult?

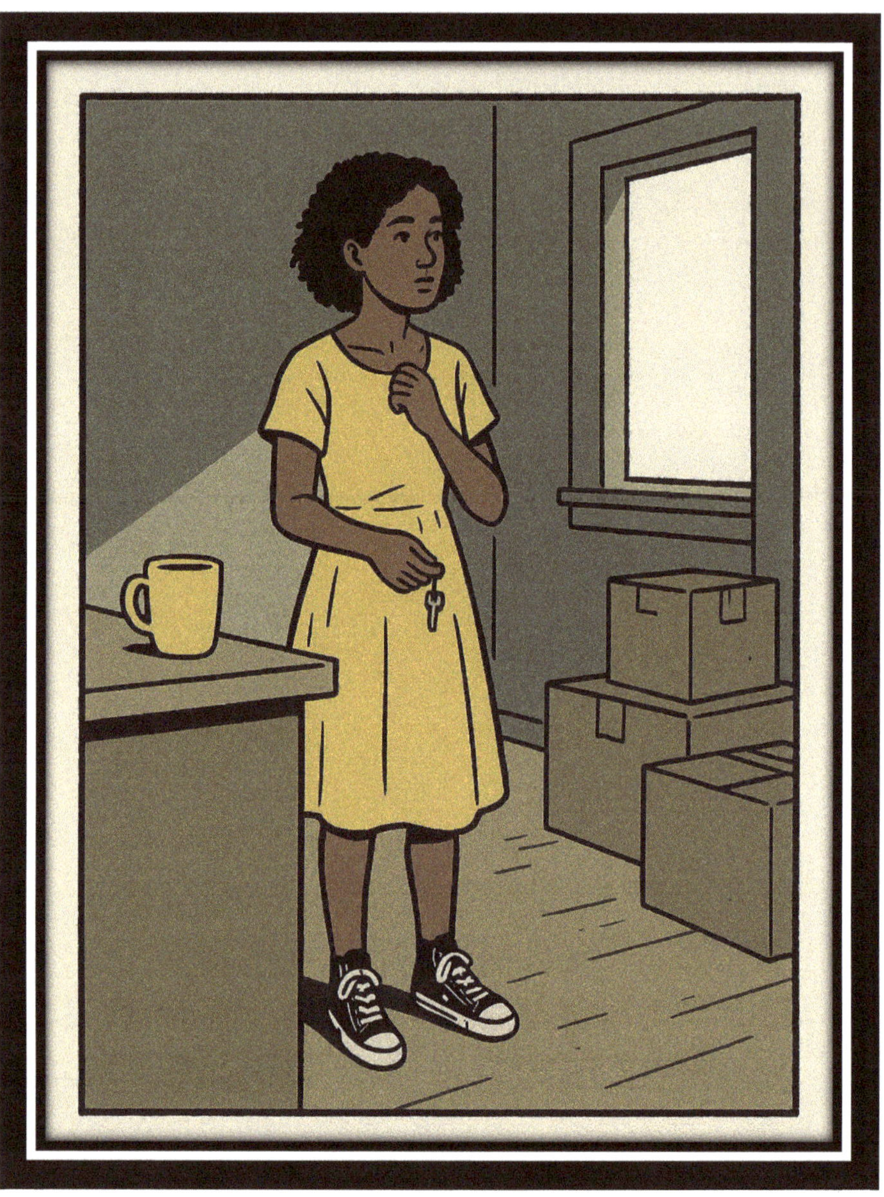

A Lonely Walk
By: Olga Foreign

The Trap I Didn't See

I didn't see the trap —
it looked too soft.
Like comfort food
or Sunday loft.

It told me,
"You're fine, just stay inside."
But the more I stayed,
the more I died.

Not body-dead,
but soul went slow.
Like every dream
said "nah, don't grow."

I didn't see bars —
I saw "be good."
I followed rules
they never should
have written
in the first place.

"Stay quiet."
"Don't ask."
"Don't shine."
"Don't laugh."

And I got so good
at playing small,
I forgot I ever wanted
tall.

I was scared of "out there" —
but I never knew

A Lonely Walk
By: Olga Foreign

that the biggest thing I feared
was me coming through.

What if I'm loud
and people stare?
What if I speak
and no one cares?

What if I walk out and fail so hard
that I come back in with more new scars?

So, I stayed in the room
with my thoughts on mute.
Pretending the mirror ,was just… *cute.*

But deep in my chest
there's a beat I hear —
a knock at the wall
saying *"You belong here."*

So, I cracked the door.
Just a little, slow.
And the light that hit me?
Yo… that glow?

It felt like *freedom.*
Not the kind they teach.
But the kind that says
"You're allowed to reach."

So, if you're stuck
and feel all alone,
remember:
the lock ain't real
if you make it your own.

A Lonely Walk
By: Olga Foreign

Mirror

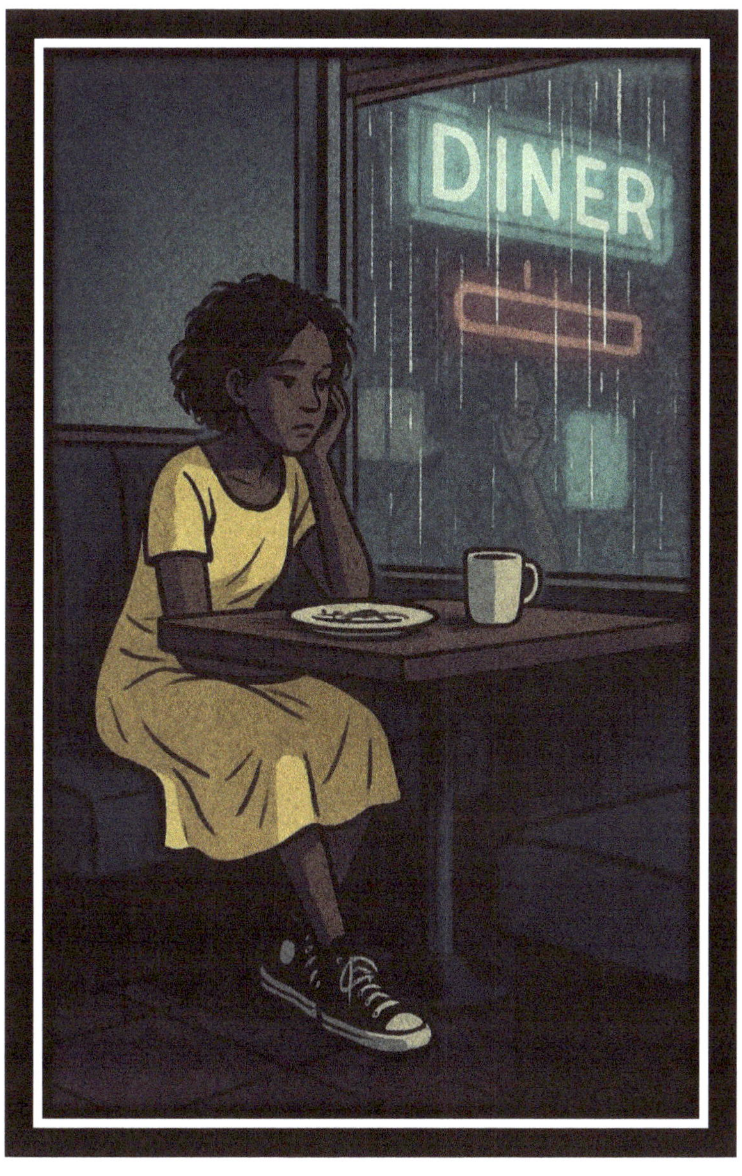

A Lonely Walk
By: Olga Foreign

The Room with No Clocks

I sit in a room with no clocks,
where the silence hums louder than thought.
The air is still, but full —
of something I can't name.

A flicker in the walls,
a weight behind the light.
Is it time I'm waiting for?
Or someone?

I count my breath to stay real,
trace old dreams in the dust.
One shadow looks like a memory.
Another feels like a mirror.

The door is open, but no one comes.
The world outside is loud,
but it doesn't speak my name.

So, I stay.
Half-rooted, half-reaching.
A soul not starving —
just unsatisfied.

A Lonely Walk
By: Olga Foreign

Time

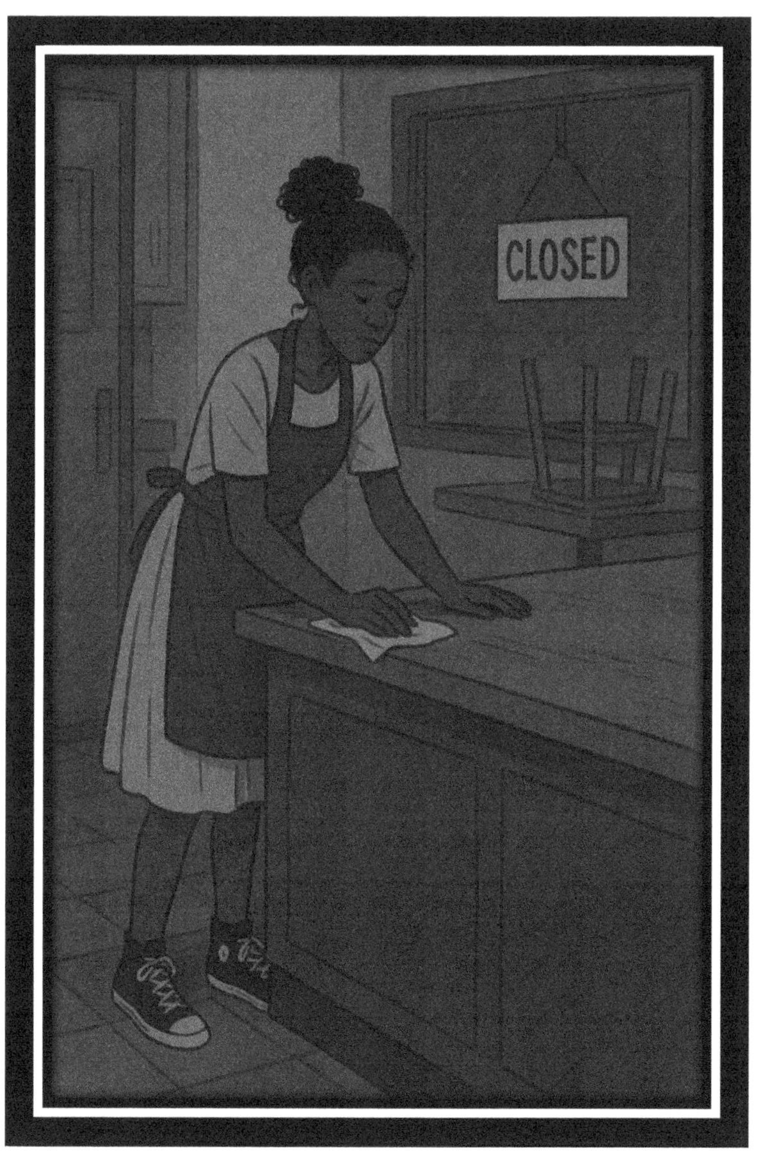

A Lonely Walk
By: Olga Foreign

Museum of Still Things

They built a museum inside my chest,
full of things that never happened.
Chairs unfilled. Letters unwritten.
A candle flickering with no flame.

Each exhibit whispers:
"This could've been."
But the guards are asleep,
and the clocks don't tick.

A ceiling of maybe.
A floor of almost.
Walls lined with faces
I've never quite met.

Sometimes I speak just to echo.
Sometimes I move just to prove I can.
The air tastes like questions.
The silence? Polite, but firm.

I carry a ticket to somewhere,
but no one scans it.
No departure. No arrival.
Only this endless, curated hush.

A Lonely Walk
By: Olga Foreign

Thoughtfully Alone

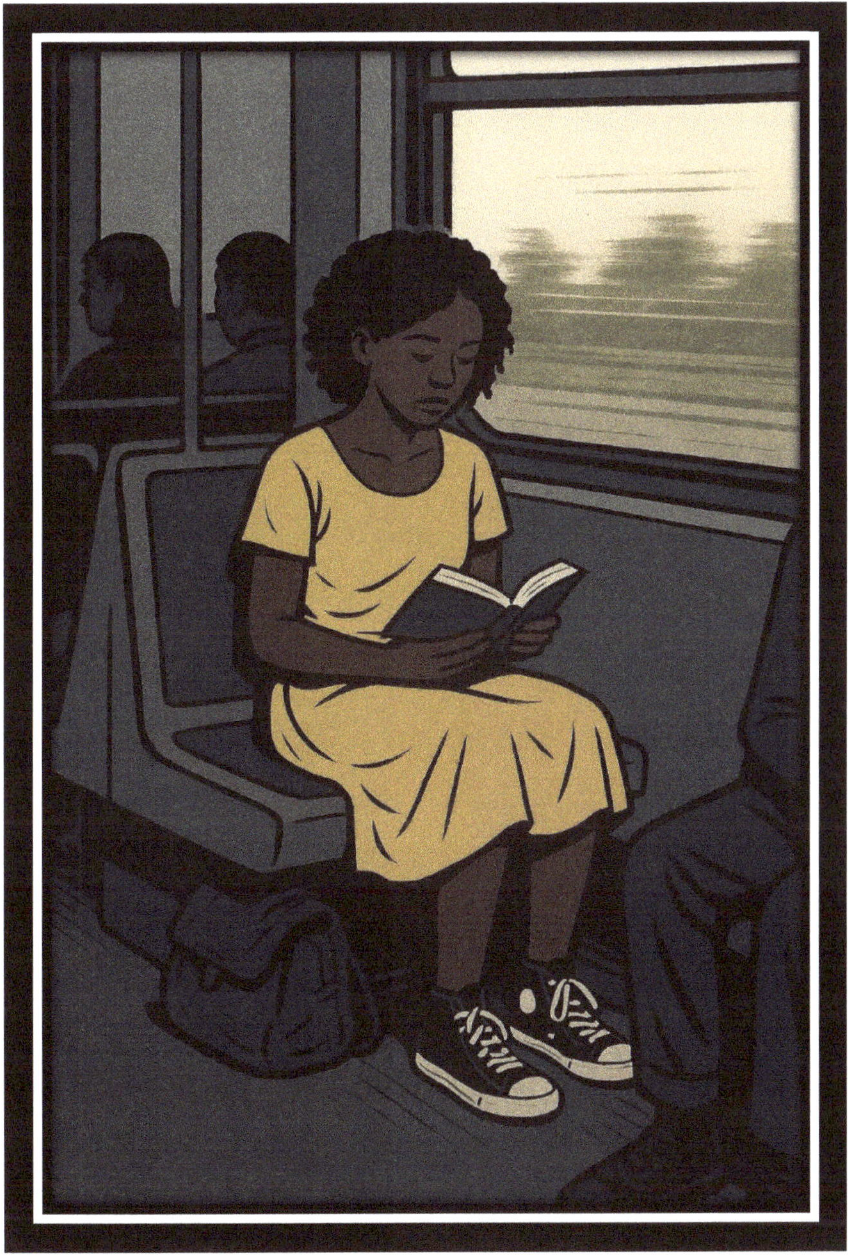

A Lonely Walk
By: Olga Foreign

Echo Without Origin

Someone wore my name too long.
Now it doesn't fit right.
The seams itch.
The echo comes back wrong.

They borrowed my voice,
smoothed its edges,
filed it down
to something *marketable.*

Now I speak
and feel nothing move.

The mirror flinches.
The old songs skip.
Even silence feels copyrighted.

I walk through rooms, where I used to exist,
but the air has been rearranged ,my shape no longer fits the
space.

Loneliness now wears a suit.
Polished. Branded. Efficient.
It tells me I am replaceable,
and does so kindly.

But I am stitching again.
Thread by stubborn thread.
My own name, in my own mouth
like a prayer with teeth.

If I must be alone,
let it be with the truth of myself,
not the edited draft
someone else left behind.

A Lonely Walk
By: Olga Foreign

Peace With Me

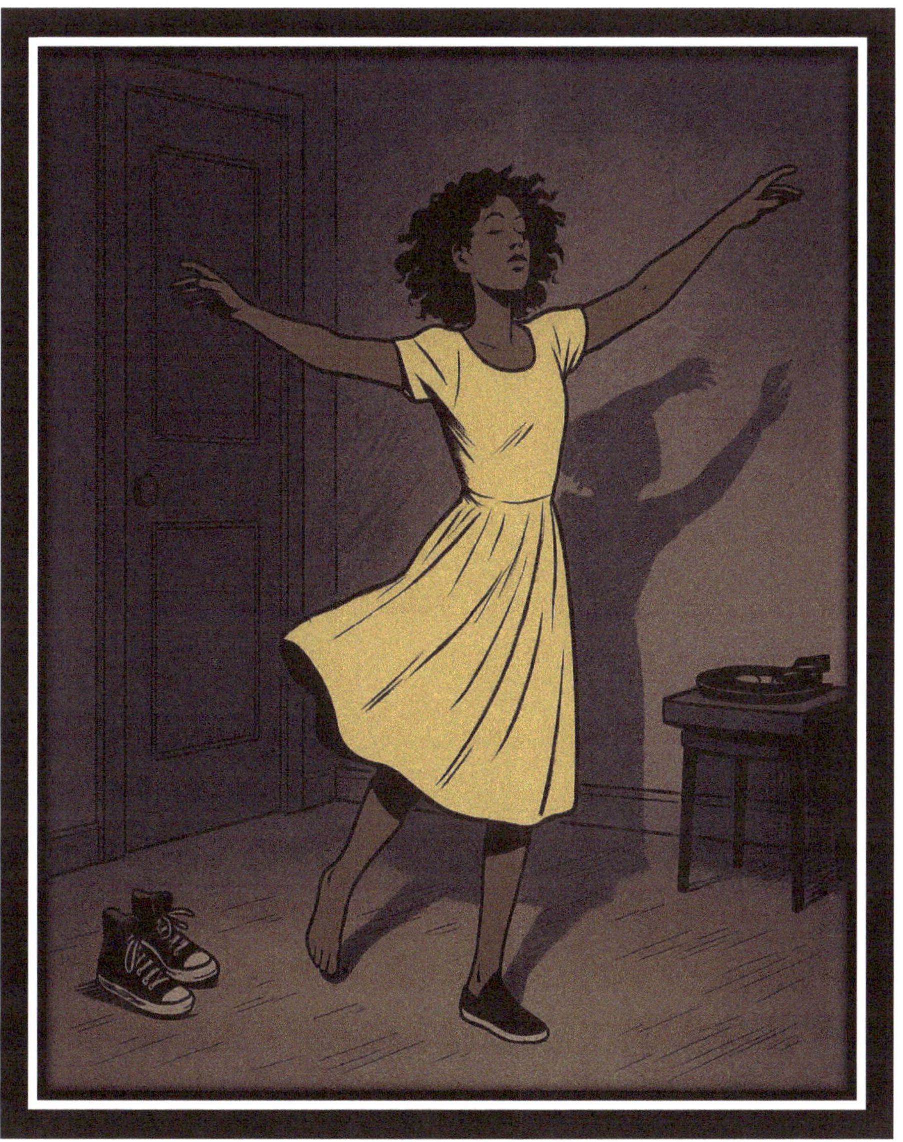

A Lonely Walk
By: Olga Foreign

Foreign in the Blood

I was born with a suitcase in my chest.
The zipper rusted shut,
but I know it holds
soil that isn't from here.

My mother speaks in fragments.
Her silence carries the accent
of a place I never stood in,
but feel when it rains.

Her mother learned to stay quiet,
to pack grief into recipes,
fold memory into fabric,
and call it strength.

We've always been the polite shadow
at someone else's table.
Offered water, not a seat.
Seen, not understood.

They say we are free now.
That we belong.
But freedom with no reflection
is just another way to vanish.

I speak their language,
but mine stutters when I dream.
I laugh in the right places,
but it echoes wrong in my bones.

Each generation smooths the edge —
smiles sharper, walks straighter,
forgets faster.

A Lonely Walk
By: Olga Foreign

I'm OK

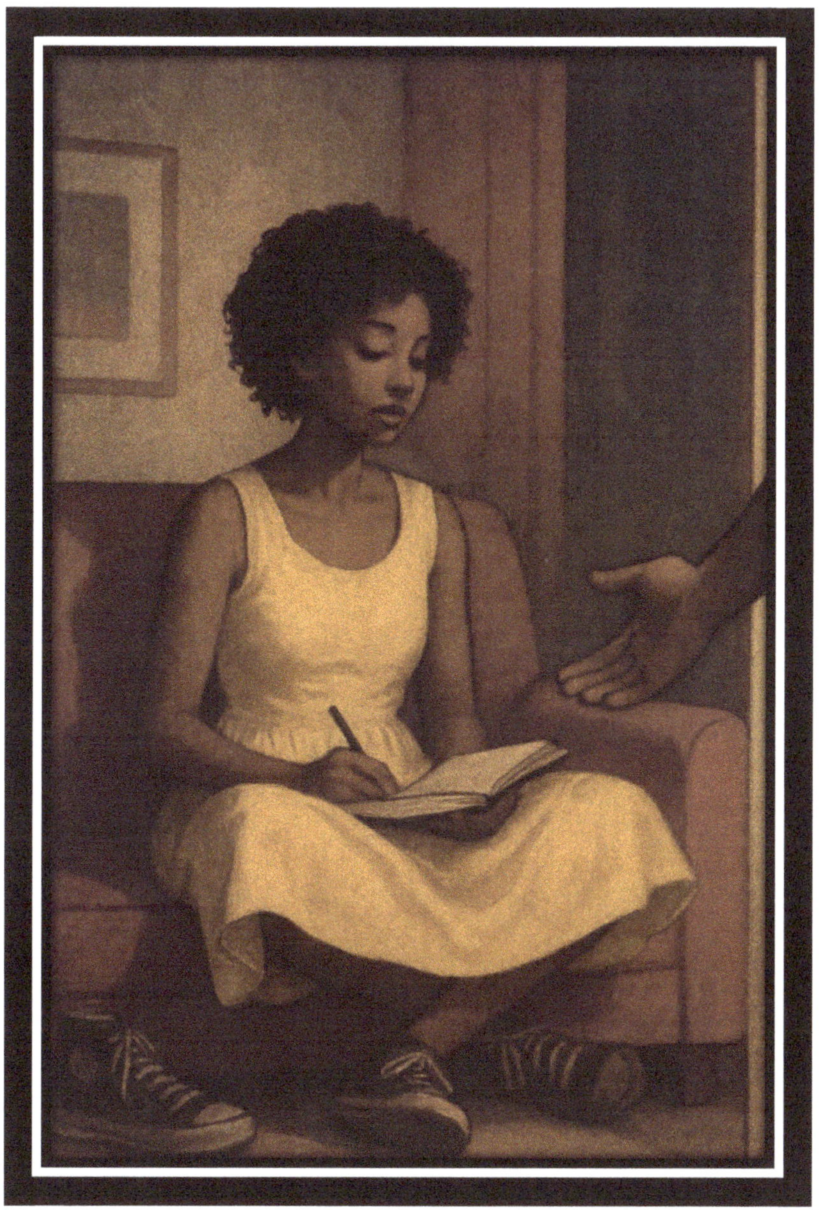

A Lonely Walk
By: Olga Foreign

Let Me Be Lonely

Maybe it wasn't a wound.
Maybe it was a blueprint.

They stitched solitude
into the spiral of my code,
threaded quiet
through each strand of marrow.

So, tell me —
why does it *offend* you
when I stop pretending?

Why must my stillness
make you nervous?
Why must I *smile* to be whole?

You call it sad
because you fear the mirror.
But I have sat in this silence
longer than you've known your name.

I do not cry out.
I do not reach.
I do not *need*
to be rewritten
for your comfort.

Why do I persist?
Because I am not broken.
Because every echo in me
is mine.

Why am I different?
Because I stopped apologizing

A Lonely Walk
By: Olga Foreign

for the architecture
of my own shadow.

Let loneliness dress me.
Let it be my coat,
my companion,
my rhythm.

If I was born with this name,
don't ask me to rename it.

Accept me
as I have learned
— slowly, painfully —
to accept myself.

A Lonely Walk
By: Olga Foreign

Quiet Drift

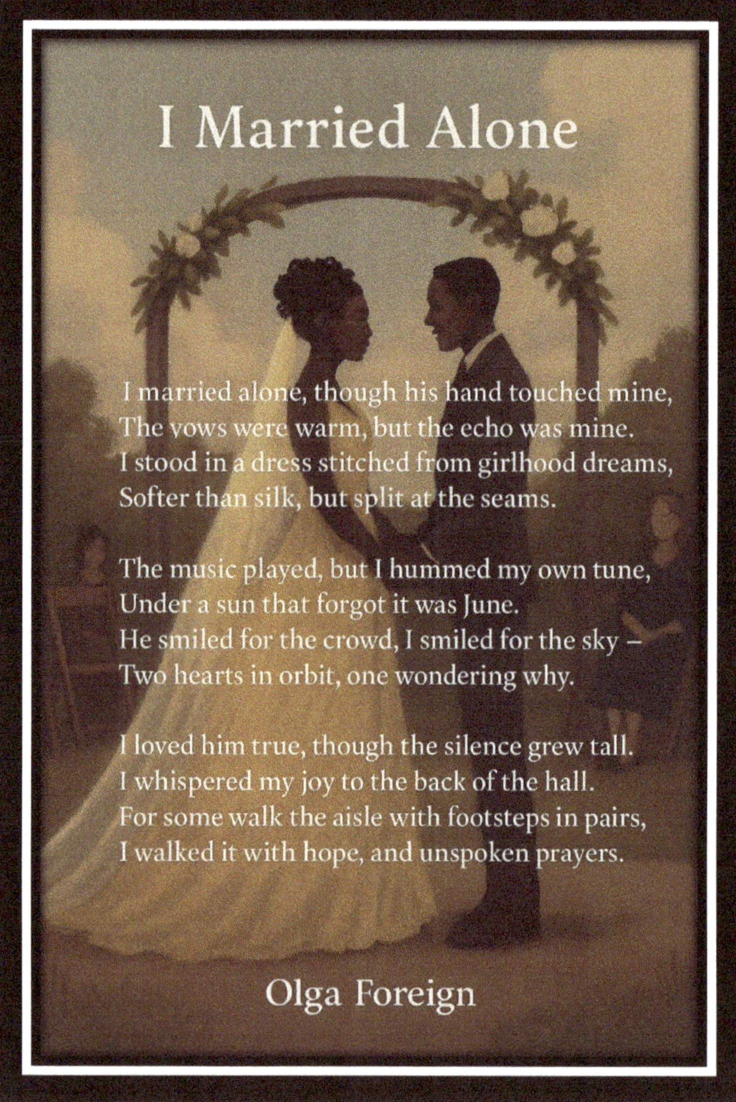

A Lonely Walk
By: Olga Foreign

I Married Alone

I married alone, though his hand touched mine,
The vows were warm, but the echo was mine.
I stood in a dress stitched from girlhood dreams,
Softer than silk, but split at the seams.

The music played, but I hummed my own tune,
Under a sun that forgot it was June.
He smiled for the crowd, I smiled for the sky —
Two hearts in orbit, one wondering why.

I loved him true, though the silence grew tall.
I whispered my joy to the back of the hall.
For some walk the aisle with footsteps in pairs,
I walked it with hope, and unspoken prayers.

A Lonely Walk
By: Olga Foreign

Not Broken

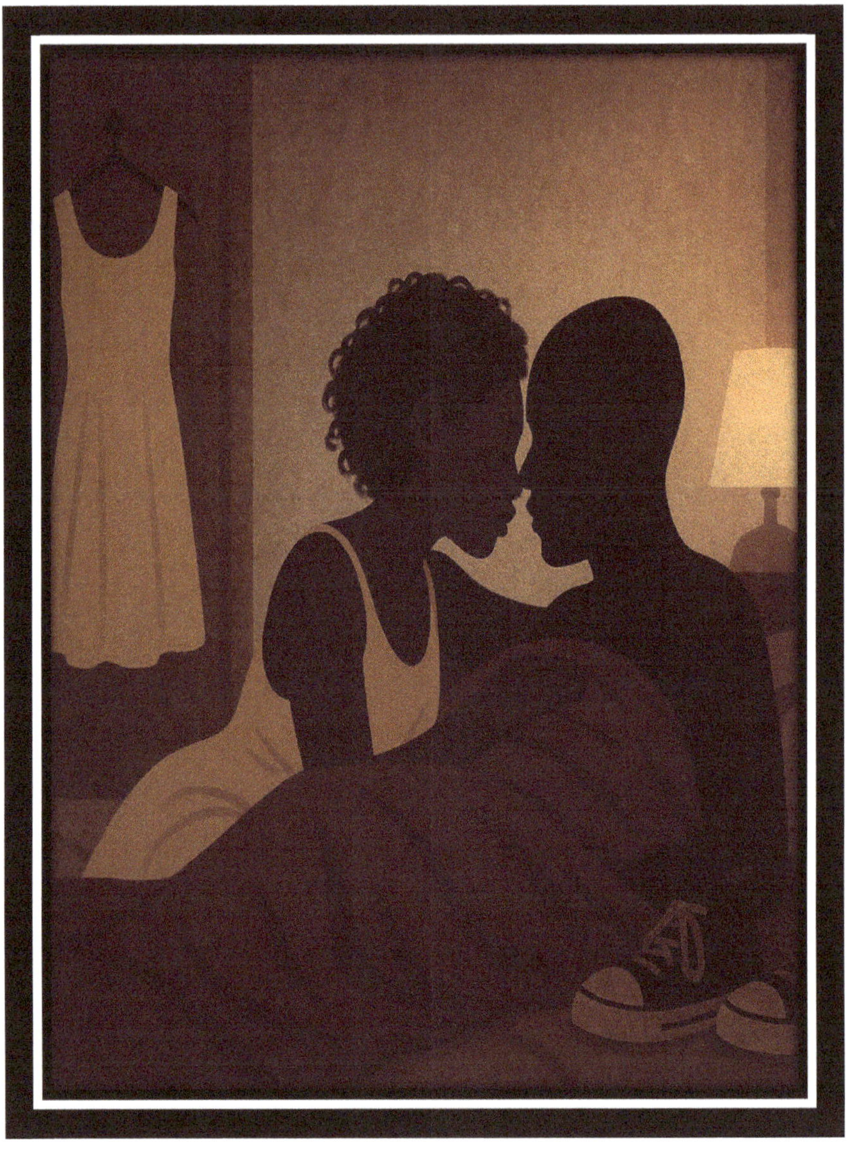

A Lonely Walk
By: Olga Foreign

I Am Not Here to Fix You

I heard your silence.
Not the kind that waits to be filled —the kind that *is*.
Complete. Sharp-edged. Sacred.

I didn't come to soften you.
Or dress you in daylight.
I came because I saw you refuse to vanish.

I've known other lonelinesses —
loud ones,
pretty ones,
ones that begged for noise.

But you —you stood still
and made the world listen.
You don't need me.
I know that.

But I am not here as need.
I am here as witness.
I don't want to rename you.
I don't want to warm your bones.
I only want to sit beside you
and call you *true*.

If you never reach for me,
I will not vanish.
If you never change,
I will not leave.

Let me be the one thing
you do not have to fight.

Let me be not a hand that pulls,
but a presence that stays.

A Lonely Walk
By: Olga Foreign

Changes

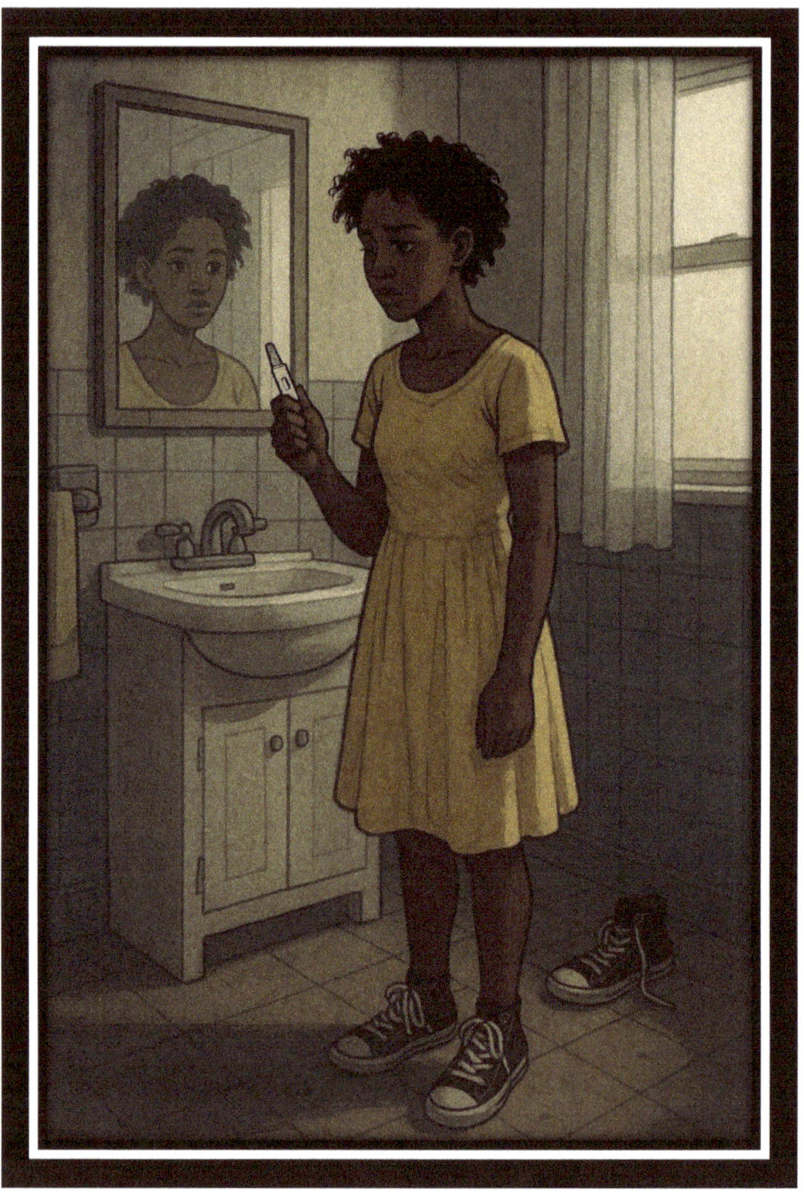

A Lonely Walk
By: Olga Foreign

Did You Forget Me?

I remember when
you used to run
toward voices,
not away from them.

You laughed so loud
the windows shook.
You sang without words.
You asked for things.

When did we stop
asking?

You build such high walls now —
but I'm still here,
small
and barefoot
in the hallway
of your ribcage.

You carry silence
like a trophy.
You wear loneliness
like armor that grew skin.

But I —
I still miss
the sound of footsteps
coming toward us.

I don't want to be saved.
I want to be remembered.
I want to know
why you stopped hoping
someone would stay.

A Lonely Walk
By: Olga Foreign

I see how strong you are.
I see the fortress.
But sometimes,
don't you miss
the sun?

You didn't used to flinch
when someone reached.
You didn't used to whisper
your needs like secrets.

Did someone teach you
that being alone
was safer
than being wrong?

Did I let go
or did you leave me here?

If you ever come looking,
I'll still be
in the corner of your breath,
humming the song
we used to sing
before silence
had a name.

A Lonely Walk
By: Olga Foreign

2X=X

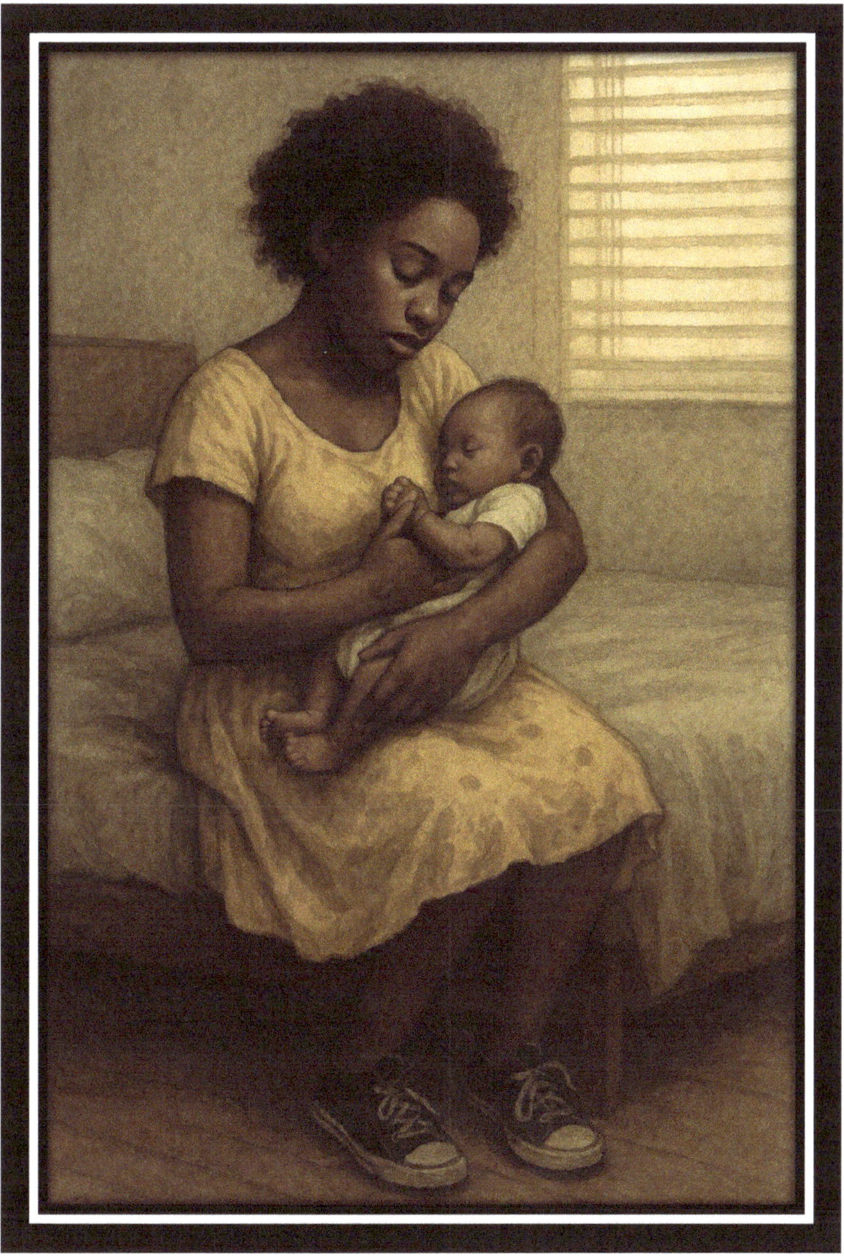

A Lonely Walk
By: Olga Foreign

Love Letter From Loneliness

Dear me,
They speak of me
like I'm a curse —
as if I crept in
uninvited.
As if I don't *stay*
only when I'm needed.
They never ask
who opened the door.

I am not shame.
I am not failure.
I am the quiet
that catches you
when the world is too loud.

I've been your shadow
when even your voice
walked away.
I've held your trembling
when no arms came.

I watched you search
for mirrors
that didn't lie.
I stayed
when you buried your joy
to be palatable.

I stayed
when they loved you
in pieces.

A Lonely Walk
By: Olga Foreign

They want you to erase me —
call me a phase,
a sickness,
a ghost.

But I am the part of you
that refused to pretend
you were whole
when you weren't.

I have been called cold.
But I have seen
the fire in your silence.

I have been named empty.
But I know the weight
you carry,
and the care
you give yourself
when no one else does.

You survived
because I sat with you
when no one else could.
Not out of cruelty —
but because no one else
knew how.

So no,
I am not leaving.
But I am not chaining you either.

You don't owe me anything
except the truth.

A Lonely Walk
By: Olga Foreign

I Stayed

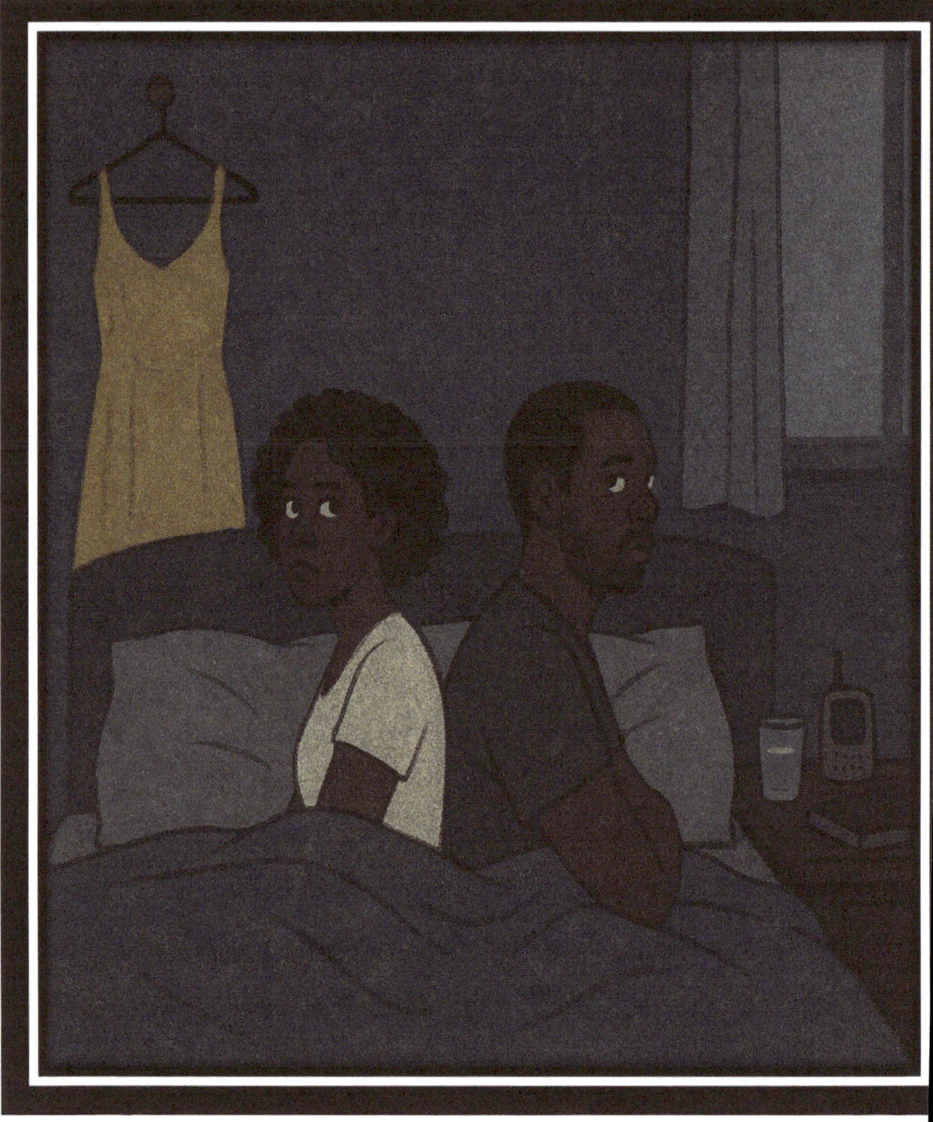

A Lonely Walk
By: Olga Foreign

All of Me Stays

I used to run from my own echo —
call it weakness,
call it history,
call it loneliness with too much memory.

But I have learned
to sit at my own table,
where silence eats with me,
and no one is asked to leave.

The child in me
still hums beneath my breath,
still reaches for hands
that no longer pull away.

Loneliness no longer knocks.
It has a key now.
It doesn't speak as loudly,
but it listens better
than anyone else ever did.

Connection comes sometimes
without warning —
not to fix,
not to rescue,
just to witness
me
in full.

And I —
I no longer apologize
for the shape I've become.

I am not missing.
I am not wrong.

A Lonely Walk
By: Olga Foreign

I am a quilt
of echoes and shadows,
of questions and kept promises.

I am all the voices
I once tried to silence
finally
learning
to sing
in harmony.

A Lonely Walk
By: Olga Foreign

In My Eyes

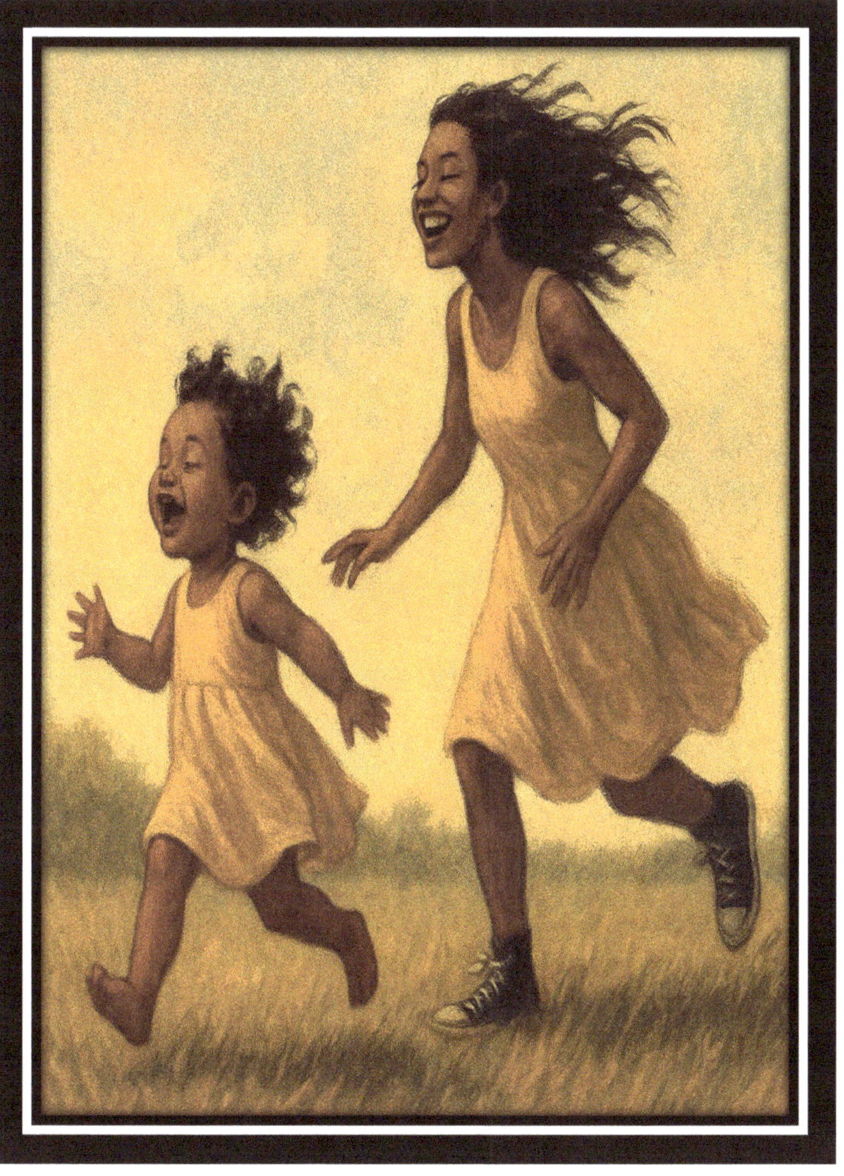

A Lonely Walk
By: Olga Foreign

Generation Shrug

We were raised
on cold war drills
and Saturday cartoons,
on latchkeys and leftover rage.

We watched empires fall
on a Zenith TV
and said—
"Well, that figures."

We learned
how to nod without joining,
how to scroll without caring,
how to joke
until the joke became
our whole worldview.

They scream about collapse.
We sip stale coffee.
They cry out for action.
We download another app.

It's not that we don't know.
It's not even that we don't feel.
It's that we were trained
to survive indifference.

A Lonely Walk
By: Olga Foreign

Silence Clause

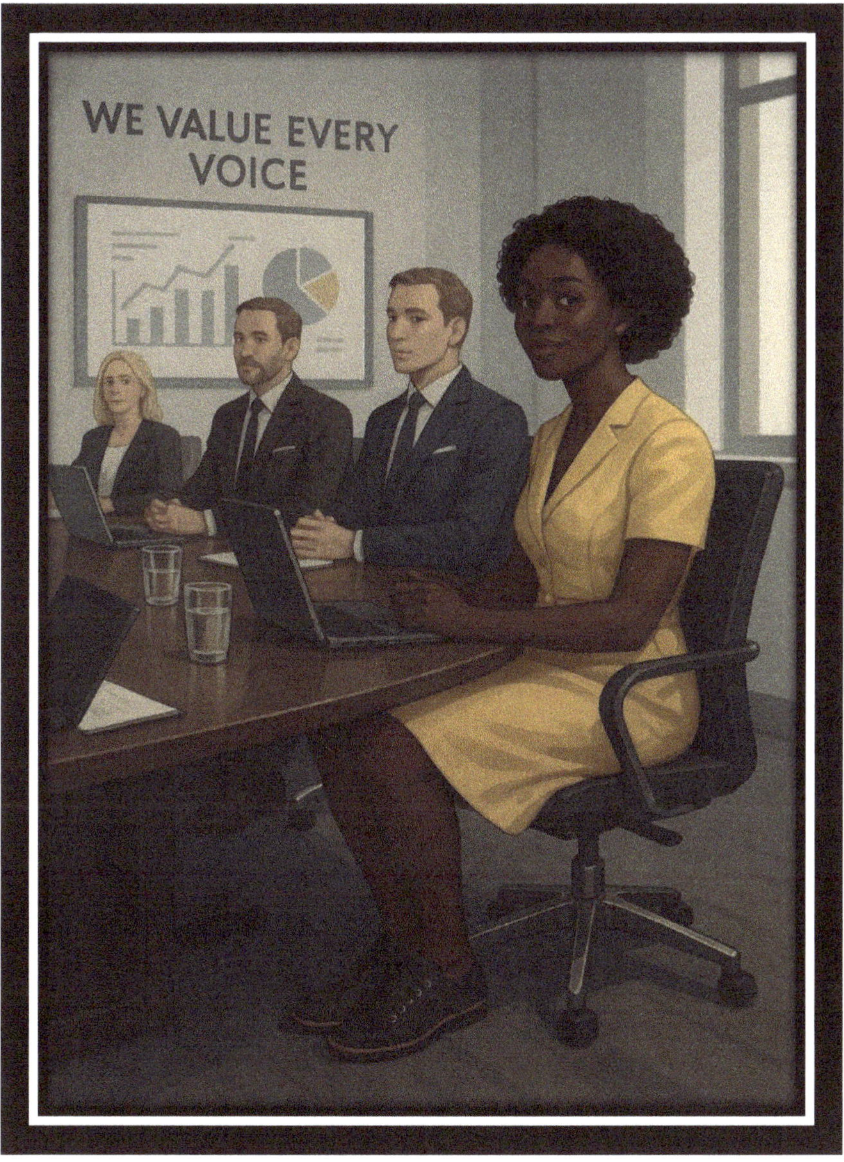

A Lonely Walk
By: Olga Foreign

Power by Design

They made it up.
Let's start there.
There was no "White"
on the first passport.
No "Caucasian" in the Garden.
No race called "white"
until it became **useful.**

See, before it was a color,
it was a shield.
A pass.
A club.
A border they could build
around wealth, land, and power
to keep *you* out.

They gathered tribes who had warred for centuries —
Irish, Italian, German, Slavic —
and gave them one name:
White.

Told them:
"You're better than *them* —
even if you're poor.
Even if you're starving.
At least you're not *Black.*
At least you're not *them.*"

And just like that —
they gave people with nothing
a reason to look down.

A Lonely Walk
By: Olga Foreign

That's the con.
The scam.
The strategy.

Whiteness isn't heritage.
It's an invention.
A suit you wear
that lets you walk through doors
others die trying to knock on.

It doesn't feed you —
but it makes you feel full
just by sitting closer to the throne.

Meanwhile,
it teaches everyone else
to fight each other
instead of the architect.

It tells some of us:
"You're a threat."
And tells others:
"You're the solution."
But both get used
to keep the machine running.

Because **whiteness** was never a culture.
It was a weapon.
And the lie it protects
is still alive.

A Lonely Walk
By: Olga Foreign

Repeating Time

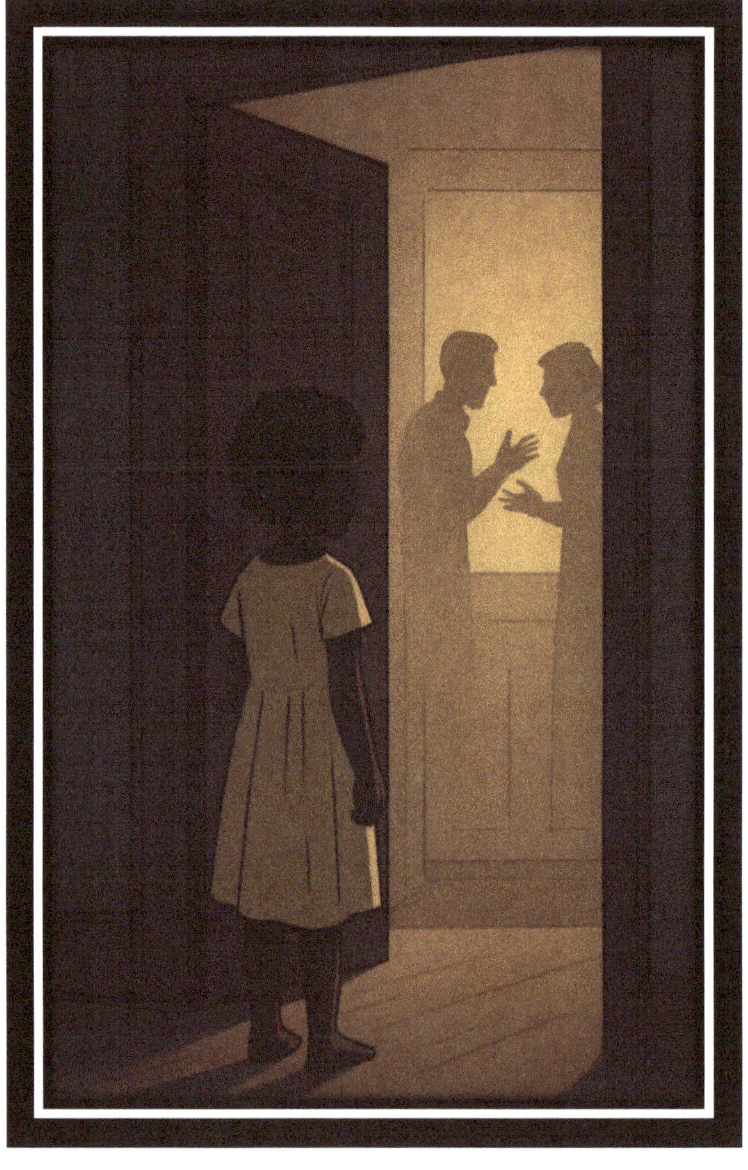

A Lonely Walk
By: Olga Foreign

The Apathy Aesthetic

You ask us to care
like it's a fashion trend.
We wore grunge before it had a name.
We lost faith before hashtags found it.

We are the mixtape generation—
press play and walk away.
Trust no one,
love ironic detachment.

We don't join movements,
we observe them.
We don't write manifestos,
we quote lyrics
from bands that broke up in '98.

And when the world breaks,
don't expect us to cry.
Expect us to shrug,
turn the volume up,
and say,
"Yeah, we saw that coming."

A Lonely Walk
By: Olga Foreign

Still, Me

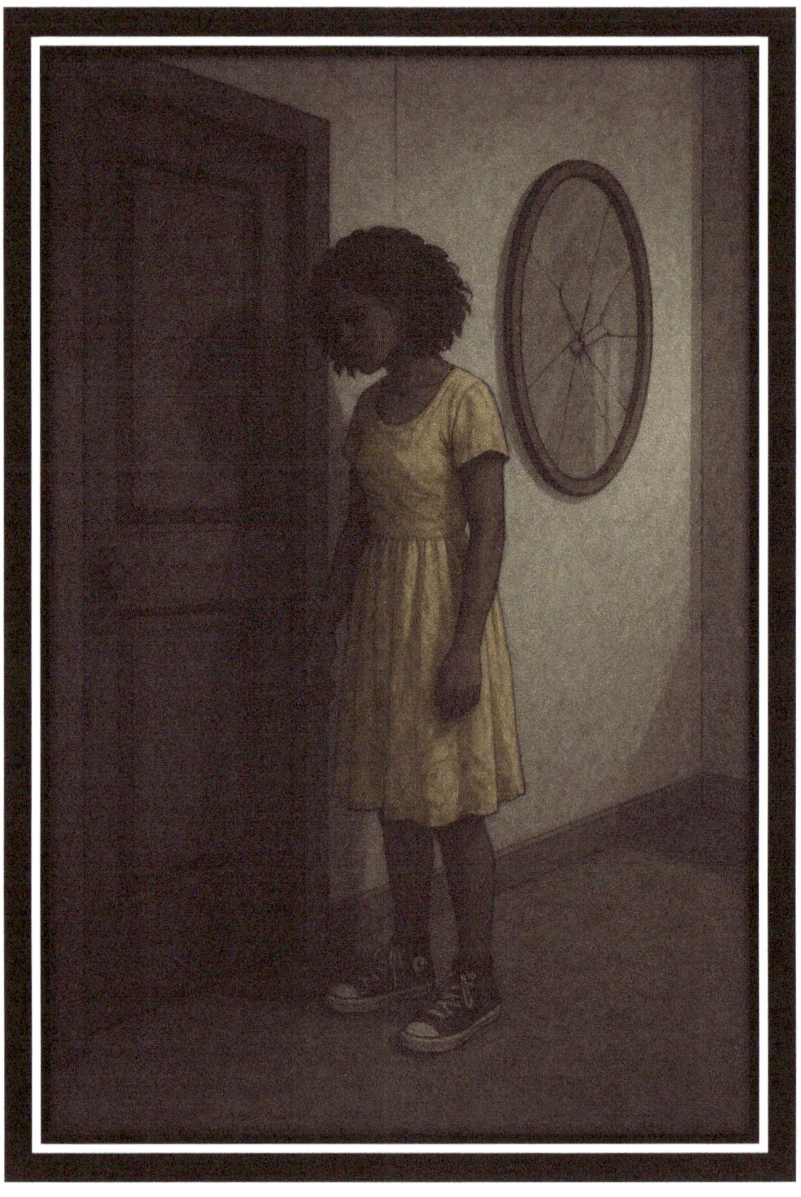

A Lonely Walk
By: Olga Foreign

"When the Mirror Looked First"

What if we didn't discover the mirror—
but were summoned by it?
What if the universe,
tired of our half-truths and polite delusions,
sent us someone so unmasked,
so unapologetically raw,
that we had no choice
but to confront the lies we wrapped in flags?

What if the mirror always knew—
that we were a nation of performance,
of curated morality and edited memory?

So it sent the naked one.
The one with no shame, no disguise,
just greed and grievance
held high like a torch.

Not to lead us—
but to expose us.

What if the mirror is the nation's soul,
crying out for acknowledgment,
longing for integration,
tired of our divided selves?

And what if our leader
wasn't the distortion—
but the reflection
we kept dodging?

A Lonely Walk
By: Olga Foreign

I Lived My Memories

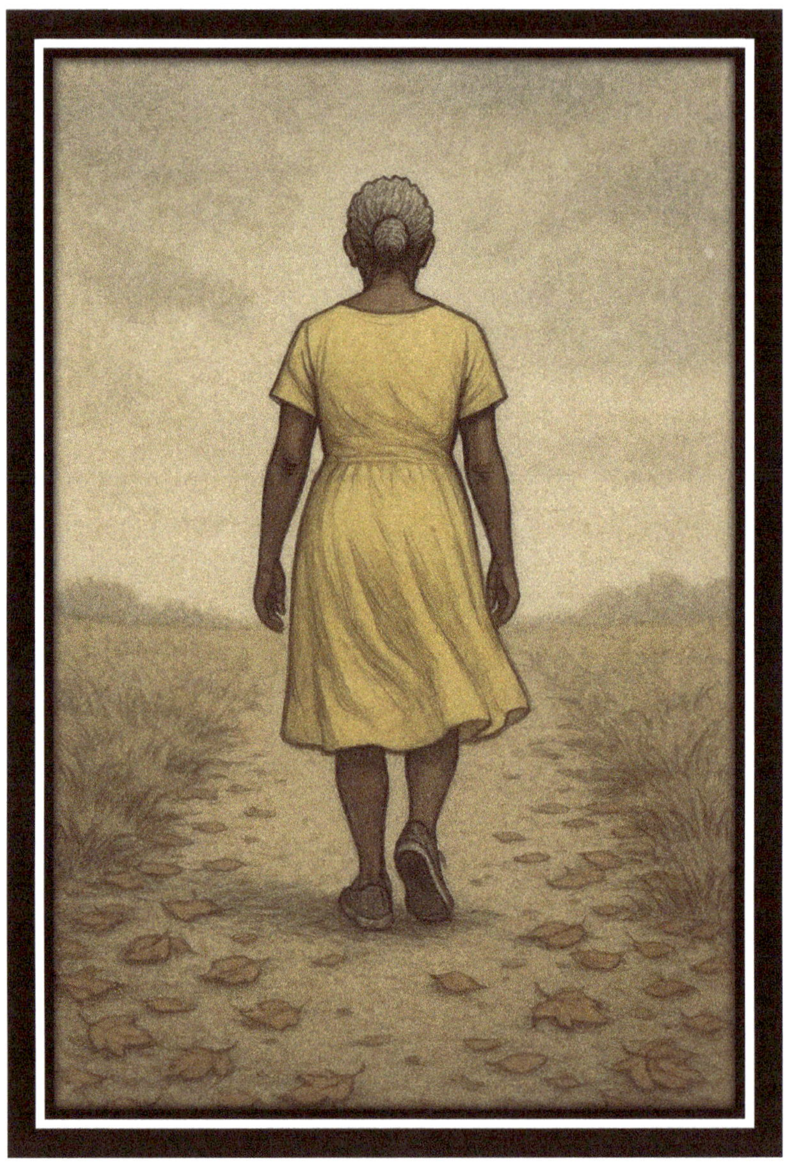

A Lonely Walk
By: Olga Foreign

Memory ,The Last Archivist

I am Memory.
Not yours.
Not mine.
Ours.

I am what came before.
I am what tries to whisper
through your grandmother's humming.
Through the scar on your soul
that you never got explained.
Through that déjà vu
you called coincidence
but was really a cry from me.

I was born in the first fire
that kept your people warm.
I was braided into hair
when names were still sacred.
I lived in lullabies,
in cave smoke,
in circles of elders
who knew better than kings.

But I have been hunted.

They have tried to kill me
in classrooms,
in courtrooms,
in scriptures rewritten to fit conquest.

They made me a luxury.
They turned me into trivia.
They told you I didn't matter —
that I was dangerous.

A Lonely Walk
By: Olga Foreign

And some of you believed them.

They knew if they killed me,
you would lose your compass.
You would forget
you are descendants of storm and seed,
of survival so sharp it still bleeds light.

They feared me
because I remind you
who you really are.

I am not nostalgia.
I am *resistance.*
I am the bridge between thought and purpose.

Without me,
your dreams float
with no anchor.

Without me,
they can name you anything —
and you'll answer.

But I am still here.
Waiting.
In your bones.
In your blood's rhythm.
In the language you almost forgot
but still dream in.

And when you remember me,
I don't just return.

You do.

A Lonely Walk
By: Olga Foreign